Original title:
The Sun, the Sea, the Tropics

Copyright © 2025 Creative Arts Management OÜ
All rights reserved.

Author: Harrison Blake
ISBN HARDBACK: 978-1-80581-672-0
ISBN PAPERBACK: 978-1-80581-199-2
ISBN EBOOK: 978-1-80581-672-0

Emerald Waves and Saffron Skies

Waves giggle and roll in playful leaps,
Splashing laughter as the shoreline sleeps.
Seagulls jest in their aerial ballet,
As crabs tap dance in their silly display.

Bright oranges swirl with shades of green,
The beach is a canvas, a happy scene.
Umbrellas wave like flags of delight,
While sunburned tourists cause a comical fright.

Sol's Dance on Liquid Glass

The warmth waltzes across smooth terrain,
While flip-flops squeak like a warped refrain.
Mermaids laugh, but they're just kids in masks,
As quicksand turns to laughter-filled tasks.

Paddleboards tip, folks splashing about,
Their graceful attempts bring giggles throughout.
Tanned legs tangled like spaghetti at best,
Chasing beachballs is a comedic quest.

Lush Breezes and Sunlit Trails

Palms sway lazily, in a chatterbox breeze,
While picnickers argue over sandwich fees.
A flock of tourists forget their sunscreen,
And end up looking like lobsters unseen.

Coconut drinks spill with a giddy cheer,
While locals roll their eyes, but never jeer.
Flip-flops fly as children make a dash,
It's a parade of laughter with every splash.

Reflections of a Bright Horizon

The horizon stretches, a colorful tease,
While sunburned grumps complain with a sneeze.
Fishermen brag of tales from the deep,
In reality, they only caught a sleep.

Beach balls bounce in a jolly ballet,
As sunscreen bottles get guzzled away.
Everyone's dancing with a twist and a fall,
While seagull spectators squawk "Not this at all!"

Golden Horizons

A bright orb peeks, not shy or coy,
Castaway dreams on a floating toy.
Crabs dance around in a silly line,
Juggling shells under palm trees' twine.

Flip-flops leap in aquatic delight,
While seagulls gossip in sheer daylight.
The coconut fell, with a thud, oh dear!
Is that laughter or a beachy cheer?

Waves of Luminous Dreams

Splashing waves call out with a cheeky grin,
"Come take a dip, let the splashing begin!"
Fish perform pirouettes, such graceful acts,
While nearby dolphins plot oceanic pranks.

A surfboard sails like a runaway kite,
With a surfer who yells, "This can't be right!"
As jellyfish float in a whimsical trance,
We laugh as they wiggle and ready to dance.

Shimmering Sands of Paradise

Sandy castles toppled by mischievous tides,
As kids throw tantrums while seagulls glide.
A crab steals a snack, quite the bold heist,
While sunscreen squirted turns into a fight!

Sunbathers rise like contented logs,
Waving at fish who swim like soggy dogs.
With umbrellas flipped upside down in a breeze,
The beach is a circus, come join the tease!

Embrace of Warmth and Water

Warmth hugs you tight like a fluffy bear,
With laughter swirling in the salty air.
Beach balls giggle, bouncing all around,
While flip-flops skip like they're on solid ground.

The hammock sways, a lazy nap's in sight,
But the gulls think it's a perch for their flight.
You chase your hat down the sunny lane,
A grand adventure, oh what a gain!

Bathed in Light Where the Waves Meet

Golden rays on laughing waves,
A crab in sunglasses struts and braves.
Flip-flops flying, a dog on the run,
While seagulls steal fries, oh what fun!

Shells whisper secrets, tides jig and sway,
A turtle in a hat leads the way.
Beach balls bounce, the kids all scream,
Margaritas spill, a sandy dream.

Carefree Laughter on Warm Breezes

Breezy hairdos, all askew,
Dancing like mermaids, happy crew.
Fruits dressed in goggles on picnic mats,
An octopus juggles with three cool hats.

Kites doing loop-de-loops in the air,
While a toad in flip-flops jumps without care.
Sandy sandwiches, laughs galore,
Bug spray disco, who could ask for more?

Tides of Time and Glimmers of Day

A clock made of driftwood, time flies by,
With fish wearing ties, oh my, oh my!
Jellyfish glide in a waltzing team,
While surfboards challenge each other to dream.

Seashells ring like phones from afar,
As a dolphin laughs—what a weird bazaar!
Sandcastles crumble, yet spirits stay bright,
Competitions of laughter, such pure delight.

Rhythms of Splendor and Tropical Ease

Mangoes swing to the bongo beat,
While parrots in jackets can't be beat.
Swimmers slide down banana boat trails,
And coconuts laugh while sharing their tales.

Tiki torches dance in a breeze so sly,
As a crab in a tuxedo waves goodbye.
With flip-flop tunes echoing through the night,
The dance floor's sandy, and everything's right.

Ocean's Lullaby at Dawn

Whispers of water dance ashore,
Waves giggle, splashing more and more.
Seafoam tickles toes in delight,
Shells gossip secrets, oh what a sight!

Napping crabs in their cozy burrows,
Chasing each other, clumsy like sparrows.
The horizon stretches, yawning wide,
As fish in bow ties swim side by side!

Seagulls sing in a pitch so silly,
While beach balls bounce and act so frilly.
The ocean hums a jovial tune,
Bringing giggles to morning's bloom!

Driftwood and Diamonds on Waves

Driftwood lounges, sunbathing still,
While jellyfish swagger, oh what a thrill!
Stars sparkles dance on the water's face,
Sandcastles wobble, not winning the race!

Footprints lead to where laughter flows,
While starfish giggle, tickling their toes.
Plastic flamingos parade with flair,
Winking at crabs that just can't compare!

Seashells clink like a tiny band,
Playing silly songs on the warm sand.
Gone are the worries, it's time to play,
In this salty comedy of the day!

Golden Glow of the Endless Day

Bananagrams bloom where the yellow meets blue,
Palm trees twirl like dancers, how do you do?
Sunscreen slip-ups, oh what a sight,
As flip-flops fly in a playful flight!

Mangos whisper gossip under the shade,
While dolphins dive and never are afraid.
Seashells and giggles fill the air,
With jokes from the tide that we all can share!

Tanned sandwiches laugh as they toast,
While watermelon winks and brags the most.
In this golden hours, we skip and sway,
In a land where silliness sweeps us away!

Island Heartbeats Beneath a Blue Sky

A ukulele strums a tune so bright,
While coconut clowns steal all the light.
Palm fronds tickle and tease in the breeze,
As laughter floats high with the swooping geese!

Bikini tops argue over last year's style,
While sandy toes dance on the shore with a smile.
Cranky crabs pinch for the best sun spot,
But the rubber duckies are all that they've got!

Tropical treats, oh what a feast,
As fruity drinks bubble, joy never ceased.
In this lively paradise, we can't help but sigh,
Hearts beat to music beneath a bright sky!

Vibrant Dances in Ocean's Grip

Waves splash and play, oh what a sight,
Crabs join the party, dancing with delight.
Seagulls squawk jokes, they dive and they swoop,
While fish throw a bash, creating a hoop.

Sandy toes wiggle, flip-flops take flight,
Beach balls are bouncing, in pure daylight.
A child starts to slip, in a comical fall,
The crowd starts to snicker, it's a festival call.

Rhythms of Dappled Light

Glittering beams make shadows come alive,
Laughter bursts forth as sunbathers jive.
Kites dance above, in whimsical cheer,
While a dog steals snacks, oh dear, oh dear!

Cool drinks are spilled, it's a bubbly affair,
Mangoes and laughter float through the air.
A surfboard tips over, with a splash and a cheer,
The beach is a circus, with everyone near.

Serene Shores and Golden Dreams

On the warm stretch of sand, a picnic takes flight,
With ants joining in, oh what a funny sight!
A sandwich goes flying, in quest for the breeze,
While a seagull plots mischief, with expert tease.

Children build castles, that tumble and fall,
As laughter erupts, it echoes through all.
Palm trees are swaying, they join the fun,
In these golden moments, we all become one.

A Tapestry of Warmth and Blue

Mermaids are giggling, with sparkles in tow,
As fish share their secrets, all set for a show.
A snorkeler's flailing, with bubbles galore,
While laughter erupts from the beach to the shore.

Bright towels are flapping, like flags in the breeze,
While sunscreen battles, bring everyone to knees.
Life's a grand joke beneath dappled skies,
With a hearty chuckle, the day softly flies.

Celestial Flames and Tropical Breezes

Golden rays dance with glee,
While seagulls squawk playfully,
Sandcastles lean, oh what a sight,
As waves crash with a splashing bite.

Beach balls bounce in merry rounds,
Sun hats fly like playful hounds,
Laughter echoes through the air,
Because it's hard to have a care!

Ice cream drips like melting dreams,
While flip-flops tease with funky schemes,
Tanned toes wriggle, oh so bright,
As beach games roll into the night.

So grab your towel and take a seat,
Where sun-kissed fun is quite the treat,
And let the joyous moments sway,
In this tropical, silly play!

Twilight Reflections in Aquamarine Depths

Beneath the waves, the fish all grin,
In coral castles, they swim and spin.
Shells wear hats; they hold a ball,
While crabs perform their grand crab crawl.

Moonlight giggles, surf's a dance,
As dolphins leap, oh what a chance!
With winks and flips, they steal the show,
Making seaweed bow low, then grow.

Starfish lounge, their arms out wide,
On sandy beaches where star dreams bide.
A jellyfish dons a fancy sash,
Wobbling slowly, oh so brash!

In this twilight's shimmer, a jest unfolds,
With laughter swirling, the night beholds.
Where nature's quirks unite and play,
In depths of mirth through night and day!

Sunlit Shores and Gentle Caresses

Bright umbrellas tilt like happy hats,
As beach bunnies dash, in playful spats.
Sandy toes make art with ease,
While gulls swoop down for leftover cheese.

Chairs recline in lazy calm,
With sunblock splashed in a funny balm.
Tanned bodies roll, oh what a sight,
Flip-flops flying in pure delight!

Snorkeling gear on heads like crowns,
As laughter bubbles, no one frowns.
Beachcombers stroll, treasures to find,
With seashells tucked in a curious kind.

A seahorse winks, and crabs do a jig,
While kids chase shadows, not too big.
In this realm where joy's the rule,
Life feels like a whimsical school!

Horizon's Kiss at Dusk

As day fades out, the sky rejoices,
Whispers of laughter are happy voices.
Fruit punch spills, a bright cascade,
While sandcastles glow, a fleeting parade.

Chill out pools echo with a splash,
While people drum up a fun bash.
With tiki torches lighting the night,
Little ones twirl, a joyous flight!

Glowworms twinkle like tiny stars,
As mermaids giggle, showing their scars.
The breeze tickles with gentle tease,
Bringing warmth like a cozy breeze.

At day's end, with a comedic gleam,
Nature laughs, and dreamers beam.
In this wild, silly, vibrant prize,
The horizon blushes, waves give rise!

Flickering Flames and Endless Horizons

Bright orbs dance in the sky,
Clumsy crabs wave goodbye.
Cocktails spill with a grin,
As sand gets stuck in our skin.

Hats fly off in the gust,
We laugh till we combust.
Barbecues turn to fairs,
While laughter fills the air.

Seagulls dive with a twist,
And snacks become a tryst.
Umbrellas dance like fools,
As we bask in our cool pools.

Whispered Wishes on a Summer Breeze

Whispers float on warm air,
Silly dreams without care.
Flip-flops squeak on the walk,
As we share laughs and talk.

Mango juice drips down chins,
The race to the waves begins.
Surfers wipe out with flair,
Splashing water everywhere!

Cats snooze in the shade,
While our antics parade.
Time ticks slow, what a tease,
Each moment feels like a breeze.

Shores of Kaleidoscopic Bliss

Pumpkins in the sand, how bizarre!
With flamingo floats, we travel far.
Sunscreen battles, a slippery fight,
Stripes and dots reflect the light.

Shells adorn our wild hats,
We pretend to be cool cats.
Find a crab with a glare,
Then we run, a grumpy pair!

Ice cream cones wobble and sway,
As seagulls scream, "Hey! Hey!"
Giggling 'til the day fades,
With a dance in our braids.

Memorable Moments Wrapped in Gold

Wear your shades like a crown,
As we tumble, splash, and drown.
Laughter echoes on the bay,
With every wave, come what may.

Sunsets give us golden cheers,
While we sip on fruity beers.
Fish frown at our loud spree,
As we catch some "oops" on the spree!

Silly hats spin on our heads,
As we dodge those pesky breads.
Moments wrapped like warm toast,
In the wackiness we boast.

Variegated Horizons at the Edge of Dream

Beneath the bright and happy rays,
Where flip-flops dance in sandy bays,
A crab in shorts with shades so wide,
Sips lemonade as waves collide.

A parrot squawks a tune so bright,
While turtles race in morning light,
With laughter echoing in the breeze,
Chasing shadows of palm trees.

The breezes swirl with mischief too,
While dolphins play a game of peek-a-boo,
As fish in bowties swim along,
A circus under nature's song.

So raise a toast to the sunlit spree,
With coconuts and giggles, you see,
In a land where mirth stretches wide,
And every wave's a playful ride.

Bright Horizons and Melodic Swells

With cocktail umbrellas that dance with flair,
A jester fish flips in salty air;
The beach ball's lost yet finds its way,
As kids giggle at the fray.

Umbrellas bloom like flowers bright,
Where laughter floats with every bite,
Seagulls join in on the fun,
Stealing fries, oh what a run!

The rhythmic splashes sing a song,
As sandcastles grow all day long.
A dog in shades, a surfer's best mate,
Chasing waves, it's never too late.

So gather 'round for sunset chimes,
With evening laughs and silly rhymes,
When stars twinkle with a giggle or two,
In this land where joy feels new.

Echoes of Joy Under Orange Dusk

When the sky bursts in shades of cheer,
A dancing lizard brings her friends near,
They shimmy and shake like it's a ball,
While crabs groove, having a ball.

As coconuts roll with a giggling sound,
They trip and tumble over the ground,
The sunset blushes with a wink,
As sipping fruit drinks makes us think.

A cat in a chair wears a floral dress,
Declares "This is my kingdom, I confess!"
With laughter ringing, and smiles so wide,
In these hues, we all can glide.

As day fades out, the stars will peek,
Revealing dreams we always seek,
In echoes of joy that never cease,
Waves of laughter, our hearts' release.

The Magic of a Timeless Paradise

Where the breeze is a tickle and the sand a hug,
A walrus wears shorts, gave a little shrug;
The palms all sway in a silly dance,
While crabs in tuxedos take a chance.

A drummer coconut keeps the beat,
As beachgoers sway, tapping their feet;
Seashells giggle with tales of their own,
While sand dancers perform, adrift and alone.

With each splash comes a chuckle and cheer,
As swimmers compete for the best cannonball here;
The sunset's show is a slapstick delight,
As day turns to night, oh what a sight!

So gather your friends for laughter and fun,
In this timeless place, we'll never run
Out of joy, as we sip and we joke,
In this paradise, where life's a golden joke.

Echoes of Distant Paradise

A parrot squawks with style,
Dancing on the palm's wide aisle.
Coconuts roll with laughter,
As tourists chase their glee soon after.

Waves whisper tales of a sleepy crab,
Who dreams of dance, not just a fab.
Flip-flops flying, oh what a sight,
Who knew sand could lead to such delight?

Tropical fruits all in a race,
Mangoes can't keep up with grace.
A hammock sways as if to tease,
Join the ride, it's sure to please!

And in the distance, a boat's small plight,
The captain's hat far out of sight.
Laugh out loud; let worries cease,
In this jolly, sandy release!

Shining Lattice of Salt and Light

Glimmers dance on surfaces bright,
While seagulls squawk, what a fright!
Holiday hats fly like dreams,
In this paradise, life's not as it seems.

Sand castles rise, but they get trashed,
By waves that giggle as they crashed.
A sunburned fellow, legs like shrimp,
Screams for shade, does the limbo limp?

Beach balls bounce in a comical spree,
As little kids giggle with glee.
Adulting's hard, they all can see,
So let's pretend we're all carefree!

Straw hats bob, a parade of fun,
Mistakes are welcome; don't shun the sun!
Grab a drink, sip slow, and say,
What a wacky, wonderful day!

Gentle Caress of the Tropic's Breath

Dancing leaves whisper secrets of cheer,
As flip-flops chat, oh so clear!
A pineapple sighs in ripe delight,
With hues of gold under twilight.

Surfboards tumble like bags of chips,
While laughter escapes sunburned lips.
Waves that wiggle, hapless and bold,
Make silly stories that never grow old.

Shells gather tales of clueless fish,
Who dream of fame and a sushi dish.
While surfers chase after shallow dreams,
A coconut rolls with sunlit beams!

Camels in shades pose for a snap,
While beachgoers stretch in a lazy nap.
Don't forget the sand in your hair,
It's a badge of honor, so don't despair!

Mesmerizing Glimmers on Brine

Rays of giggles chase shadows short,
As crabs in costumes arrive for court.
Tanned folks roll with a wink and jest,
In the warmth where worries take a rest.

A fish with swagger scoots by in style,
While sunburnt tourists cheer for a while.
Buckets and spades, oh what a mess,
Sand dollar dreams of ocean's finesse!

People stumble, umbrellas fly high,
As wind plays tag with a seagull's cry.
A sundae melts where giggles collide,
Join in the fun, let joy be your guide!

And when night falls, laughter does cling,
With sand in toes, let the fun begin!
With stars twinkling, carefree we'll sing,
In this heaven, forever we cling!

Luminous Canopy of the Isles

Beneath bright blooms, the lizards dance,
With silly hats, they prance,
Coconuts roll like marbles at play,
While parrots gossip the day away.

Tropical drinks with umbrellas sway,
Cheers to the octopus that got away,
Sandcastles crumble, the tide's a tease,
No worries here, just ocean breeze.

Fish in shades of pink and blue,
Swim past dive-bombing, brazen gnu,
Flip-flops fly as beach balls soar,
Who knew a crab could dance on the shore?

In flip-flops, we stumble and trip,
While sipping smoothies, we take a dip,
Laughter echoes through the palm fronds high,
As antics unfold beneath the sky.

Twilight's Embrace Over Calypso Waters

As roosters crow in the fading light,
Mangoes fall with a comical fright,
Dance-offs start where the shoreline bends,
We twirl, we slip, and make new friends.

Hammocks swing to the rhythm of night,
But was that a ghost or a kite in flight?
Swimmers splash while giggling hard,
The seaweed wiggles, like a dance card!

Fireflies twinkle, but watch your drink,
Is that a fish? Or is it a clink?
Mirthful shadows, we act so spry,
While moonlit jokes make the dolphins sigh.

In the warm, salty air we jest,
With clinking glasses and gregarious zest,
As stars wink down from tapestry skies,
We share our laughter, just a few good fries.

Golden Radiance Over Coral Shores

Sandy toes meet the salty tide,
With sunscreen smeared, we dance with pride,
Bikini bottoms, oh dear, what a sight,
As beach balls bounce, in pure delight!

The crabs have formed a marching band,
With tiny drums made of seashell sand,
We cheer them on with a piña colada,
Dreaming of snacks and a sunblock saga.

Splashing water, a giggling chase,
While seagulls dive with style and grace,
To steal our fries, they squawk and squirm,
As we play tag with the ocean's charm.

The sunset blushes, what a great show,
As we flip the script on a sandcastle woe,
With giggles exploding like fireworks bright,
We revel and snicker till the stars ignite.

Whispering Waves at Dawn's Embrace

Morning's glow finds us at play,
As the tide tickles our toes at bay,
A pelican lurks, looks for a treat,
While seagulls circle, oh what a feat!

Caution! A crab with a royal stance,
Challenges us to a wobbly dance,
With sunscreen smeared on our noses too,
We prance like fools, oh, who knew?

Dolphins leap with a splashy grin,
While jellyfish float, a bouncy kin,
Our laughter rings, like shells on the shore,
Making memories we'll laugh at for sure!

As daylight blooms, the skies turn bright,
With soggy sandwiches, we delight,
The day's just starting, and so are we,
With funny tales from the salty spree.

Embrace of Warm Winds and Crystal Waters

Gentle breezes tickle my toes,
While goofy clouds do silly poses.
Laughter dances on salty air,
As crabs play tag without a care.

Flip-flops flying with each swift stride,
Seagulls squawking like they're the guide.
Sandcastles lean, a wobbly show,
As waves come in to steal the dough.

Bright towels flutter like flags of cheer,
Ice cream drips; oh, what a smear!
Pineapple hats on heads say "Yo!",
While sunburned noses steal the show.

In this silly sunlit retreat,
With beach ball battles, fun's complete.
Let's laugh 'til our tummies ache,
In this sunny paradise we make.

A Tapestry of Waves and Light

A canvas where the colors blend,
With jokes that never seem to end.
Flip flops squeak, a comical sound,
As laughter echoes all around.

Jellyfish wobble, like dancers whimsy,
While kids build dreams that look quite flimsy.
Chasing crabs in a hilarious chase,
With sparks of joy lighting up the place.

Sunhats like umbrellas try to take flight,
While sunscreen battles with skin so white.
Frisbee blunders, a rescue from sea,
As tidal waves of giggles decree.

In this world where fun's the goal,
We trade our worries for playful strolls.
Each splash and laugh brings pure delight,
A brilliant dance in golden light.

Requiem of Day and the Ocean's Heart

As day takes a bow, the stars appear,
With fireflies wishing they could steer.
Waves hum tunes of sweet goodbyes,
While everyone waves from the twilight skies.

Surfboards tumble, a comic ballet,
As sunset fades to end the play.
Sunburned folks in bright attire,
Tell tales of sharks that danced with fire.

The moon peeks down, a cheeky grin,
While sandcastles sigh, "We just can't win!"
Turtles laugh as they crawl to shore,
Exchanging jokes that leave us wanting more.

So raise a toast to this zany night,
With campfire stories that feel just right.
In this folly where memories start,
A hilarious requiem for the heart.

Boundless Azure Under Fiery Splendor

Under a sky that giggles and blooms,
We sprint and dive in colorful costumes.
The pop of coconuts, a comedy show,
While sun hats spin like they're in a flow.

Underneath the waves, fish play hide and seek,
As shells and treasures laugh at the meek.
An octopus juggles, what a sight!
While surfers boogie before the night.

With laughter sparkling in the breeze,
Every moment dances, puts us at ease.
Picnic baskets tipped, food rolling away,
As pelicans steal our chips for the day.

Beneath the stars, the rhythm goes on,
With glowing tides hum a merry song.
In this vast playground where fun is spry,
We savor each moment as time slips by.

Vibrant Colors of an Endless Summer

Flip-flops squeak on sizzling sand,
A crab wearing shades, looking quite grand.
Beach balls bounce like happy kids,
While seagulls steal fries, oh the bids!

Lemonade drips down my chin anew,
I'm covered in sunscreen—a white goo.
Umbrellas bloom like odd flowers bright,
As sunburned folks grumble, 'Not quite right!'

Bright swimsuits dance in the ocean breeze,
Kids scream with glee, climbing up trees.
Tanning butter smells like popcorn delight,
And as night falls, we bid day goodnight.

With sunset hues painting the skies,
Even the crabs look a bit surprised.
We laugh till we ache, roll our eyes wide,
In this colorful world where fun can't hide.

Shores of Serenity Under Golden Glows

Sipping on coconuts, a graceful feat,
While my buddy's lost, looking for his seat.
Shells play hide and seek, what a chase,
While jellyfish float—it's a wobbly race.

Sandcastles stand like tiny great kings,
Guarded by seagulls with funny flings.
I tried to surf but ended in a flop,
The wave laughed hard—what a hilarious drop!

A tanned dog runs with a bright red bone,
He's the true master of this sandy throne.
We try to dance but stumble on our toes,
As beach attire reveals too much, who knows?

The only worries here are ice cream treats,
And whether to rerun those dance-off feats.
With twilight whispers and stars glowing bright,
We chuckle and dream of another fun night.

Chasing Sunbeams Over Tropical Isles

In a kayak race, I'm clearly the champ,
Till I get stuck with a giggly old lamp.
The fish tease me, flip-flopping away,
While I splash and scream, 'Come back and play!'

With hammock naps that never seem wrong,
My neighbor snores loud; he thinks he's a song.
Mangoes drop like comedies on my head,
As I clutch my belly, laughing in bed.

Every wave crackles with silly delights,
I dance with the foam under starry nights.
The crabs plot mischief, their little red hats,
In this wild world where the giggling spats.

So here's to life on these vibrant shores,
Where laughter spills out of open doors.
With every splash and each clumsy dive,
It's a tropical circus, and we're all alive!

Melodies of Light and Seafoam

The sound of waves is a giggling tune,
While flip-flops tap under the big, round moon.
Seagulls improvise, cracking jokes about fish,
I nod along—"That's my secret wish!"

Crafting sand pies with a random seashell,
My friend claims she's baked a cake; wish me well!
Sunscreen wars break out, it's pure delight,
As we laugh and apply with all of our might.

Toasting marshmallows that taste like squish,
We celebrate victories with every silly dish.
A crab joins the party, dancing away,
Exposing his moves in the salty ballet.

As nightfall wraps us in a cozy embrace,
We share wild tales with a wink on our face.
The sea sings songs while we sit and dream,
In this goofy paradise, life's but a gleam.

Ocean's Serenade Under Palm Fronds

A crab with dreams of fame and cheer,
Danced a jig, his friends drew near.
Seagulls cawed a mocking tune,
While fish laughed at his afternoon.

A child threw pebbles, giggles bright,
Splashing water, what a sight!
The crab did twirl, a funny feat,
Petty royalty, he felt quite sweet.

A mermaid winked, all in fun,
Puffed up a bubble, let it run.
The crab took a bow, feathers in hand,
While the audience clapped on the sand.

With every slip and every fall,
The laughter echoed, a joyful call.
Ocean's stage, with all its glee,
Who knew sea life was so zany?

Sunset's Palette on Water's Canvas

Colors burst like laughter loud,
As fish form a flippin' crowd.
A dolphin twirled in pinks and gold,
Telling stories never old.

A turtle grumbled, 'Don't be slow!'
While waves tickled, putting on a show.
The horizon blushed with a cheeky grin,
As starfish played their silly spin.

Crabs devised a game of tag,
While jellyfish floated, oh what a drag!
The scene, a riot of cheer and mirth,
Creating joy on this vibrant earth.

A shrimp with style, danced in place,
While the sun painted smiles on every face.
Together they laughed until the night,
Art from nature, a funny sight.

Warmth of Daybreak on Waving Boughs

Morning breaks, a rooster crows,
While a monkey scampers, pulling toes.
Bananas swing on swaying ropes,
Each bite coaxing morning hopes.

A sloth sighs, 'I'll move, but wait,'
As birds argue on his fate.
The warmth brings joy, who can resist?
Monkeys glimpse at the morning mist.

With laughter echoing through the trees,
A toucan juggles with such ease.
The laughter flies with every breeze,
While all the critters share the tease.

Soft light spills like syrup sweet,
While everyone joins in the beat.
Oh what fun in morning's glow,
Cheeky critters, putting on a show.

Dappled Light Among the Mangroves

In shadows dense, a party brews,
With critters donning party shoes.
The mudskippers hop, quite mad,
While all the hermits cheer, not sad.

The fiddler crabs are on a spree,
Tapping claws, so merrily.
A sneaky otter steals a snack,
Always ready for a little crack!

The sun peeks through, a curious eye,
As lizards bask and fly squirrels fly.
They chatter tales of finned delight,
Under branches, what a sight!

Giggles dance in the warm embrace,
While all the trees sway at their pace.
The mangroves hum a playful tune,
Join the fun, and laugh till noon!

Flickers of Light Beneath the Palm

Beneath the leaves, a shadow plays,
A crab dances in its clumsy ways.
With a flip and a twirl, oh what a sight,
It steals my sandwich, then scampers in flight.

The breeze kicks up, my hat takes off,
Chasing it, I tumble, then laugh and scoff.
A parrot squawks, "Catch me if you can!"
I give a chase, but he's a clever fan.

Nothing's as bright as an ice cream cone,
Until it melts, and I'm left alone.
A sticky mess drips down my chin,
A lizard laughs, "Hey, where have you been?"

The beach ball spins with a silly glee,
As kids run past, they trip over me.
Together we roll, in laughter we roll,
Under green coconuts and sun's bright soul.

Harmonies of Horizon and Wave

The rhythm of splashes syncs with my song,
As dolphins dance, they sing all day long.
Yet here comes a seagull, bold as can be,
He steals my chips, then laughs a hearty spree.

"Hey buddy, that's not cool!" I shout in vain,
He just shakes his head, then flies out of range.
A beach ball pops, and I jump in surprise,
As sand flies up and obscures my eyes.

The waves roll in with a playful cheer,
But here comes a wave, a bit too near.
It drenches my towel, my snack, and my shoes,
I laugh and declare it good fortune I'll choose!

Drifting along with a float that's quite wide,
A crab takes a seat, my companion and guide.
Together we float to the beat of the tide,
Sharing snacks with a twinkle and a playful slide.

Warm Embrace of Distant Shores

In the distance, a castle of foam takes its shape,
A kid builds a fortress, using a grape.
His mom calls him in, but he just winks,
With a bucket of shells, he's lost in his thinks.

I lounge on the sand, feeling so brave,
Until a rogue wave gives me a shave.
I squeal and I roll, covered in sea,
A sandcastle's taken a liking to me!

The starfish appears, all gooey and grand,
It whispers sweet nothings to my worried hand.
A little crab tumbles, sends kids all aflair,
As laughter erupts, they leap in the air!

Sun sets ablaze in a colorful cheer,
With juice stains and giggles, there's nothing to fear.
We dance on the shore, till our feet are so sore,
Swapping tales of our day, saying, "Give me some more!"

Sunlit Mosaic of a Coastal Life

A flick of a tail reveals a big surprise,
A fish in a mask, oh, what a disguise!
He wiggles and jiggles, just like a show,
As I sit on the beach, saying, "Where did you go?"

Little crabs sidestep, a tap dance delight,
While shells hold their breath, ready for the night.
A kite flies high, tangled up with a tree,
What a mess we're in, but oh what a spree!

The breeze carries laughter, a melody sweet,
While I'm told to watch out for the crowd on their feet.
They stomp and they slide, in a hilarious race,
While I sit back and chuckle, enjoying my space.

With drinks piled high, an umbrella in tow,
I raise up my cup, and say, "Give me some flow!"
The day fades away, but my heart beats alive,
For here in this paradise, we all thrive and jive!

Sunkissed Canopy and Isle's Allure

Under bright rays, the monkeys dance,
Palm trees sway in a lazy trance.
Crabs wear shades, looking so chic,
Laughing as fish in the lagoon peak.

Cockatoos squawk with a merry tune,
Trying to steal a slice of the moon.
Sandy toes in a flip-flop race,
Sandcastles sporting a goofy face.

Beach balls bounce with a joyful cheer,
While seagulls plot to swipe a beer.
Tanning chairs with a vibrant glow,
Everyone here steals the show.

So grab a drink with an umbrella steer,
In this place, life's always near.
With laughter and joy, the days unfold,
A light-hearted paradise, stories untold.

Waves Whispering Secrets to the Shore

Waves roll in with a giggling sound,
Shells hiding treasure all around.
The fish play tag, fins all a-flap,
While dolphins dive in a playful slap.

Sandcastles crumble, oh what a scene,
As kids throw sand, looking too keen.
Crabs do the cha-cha, a sight so rare,
While seagulls squawk like they just don't care.

In the tide pools, tales are spun,
An octopus hiding, just for fun.
Jellyfish bouncing, wearing a grin,
With every splash, let the games begin.

A beach tug-of-war with a giant kite,
Who'll win? Well, it's a silly fight!
With laughter echoing through the glow,
Secrets whisper, as the breezes blow.

Ebbing Tides of a Dreaming Coast

The tide pulls back like a joke untold,
Leaving footprints in silver and gold.
Starfish lounge, no worries today,
While sea turtles do ballet all day.

Shells come to life with giggles and grins,
While sand crabs boast about their wins.
With a wink and a nudge, the ocean gleams,
Whispers of sun-soaked, silly dreams.

Kites dance in a sky so blue,
Chasing birds who don't have a clue.
A crab wearing a hat, so proud and bright,
Cracks up the beach with pure delight.

As waters recede, the fun won't end,
It's a paradise where laughter's a trend.
In every splash, a silly cheer,
The ebbing tide brings joy near.

Radiant Moments in Paradise's Heart

A hammock sways like a happy dance,
Sunbeams sparkle, inviting a glance.
Bananas giggle, looking so ripe,
Dancers parade in a tropical type.

Drink umbrellas wave as they toast,
To silly moments we cherish the most.
Flip-flops flapping in a fashion spree,
As crabs juggle seashells for glee.

Bamboo huts wear flowers in style,
The laughter echoes for mile after mile.
Fruits in baskets taking a stand,
With coconuts telling tales so grand.

Under the stars, the laughter stays,
This joyful paradise in playful ways.
With every giggle and radiant spark,
Each moment glows—love's little hallmark.

Mellow Days in an Island Breeze

On a hammock, I did sway,
Sipping coconut all day.
A parrot squawked my name,
Birds seem to play my game.

A crab danced with delight,
Waving pincers left and right.
The beach ball flew so high,
I thought it learned to fly.

Drinks with umbrellas bright,
Caught my imagination's sight.
An octopus flipped a snack,
I waved, it waved right back.

But when it was time to dive,
My snacks flew in a jive.
Chasing fish with big, wide grins,
Turns out they're better at swims!

Cobalt Tides and Amber Hues

Waves come in with a cheer,
Splashing giggles all around here.
A seal wore sunglasses cool,
Swam around just like a fool.

Golden sands kissed my toes,
I chased footprints; where'd they go?
Seagulls stole my potato chip,
In their beaks, it took a trip.

Beach towels spread like dreams,
Sandcastles? More like schemes!
With buckets and shovels bright,
We built towers—oh, what a sight!

As sunset paints the skies,
A crab plays the wise guy.
With a flick of its own hand,
It rules over this beach land!

Lullabies of the Salted Breeze

In twilight's gentle embrace,
A dance-off with a fish takes place.
I wiggled my toes in the sand,
While a dolphin joined the band.

With waves singing sweet tunes,
Stars poking through cartoon balloons.
A starfish tried to do a jig,
But oh my, it was quite big!

Shells whispering tales of lore,
A crab knocked, begging for more.
Tales of pirates, treasure chests,
Yet all they found were fishy pests.

As night draped its velvety shroud,
We laughed, we sang, we were proud.
Fun wrapped in salty glee,
In a world without monotony!

Gilded Skies and Ocean's Embrace

Under soft pillows of light,
Jellyfish gliding, oh what a sight!
They bounce like balloons so high,
I can't help but question, why?

A surfer with a green wig,
Riding waves with a wiggly jig.
His board did flips and twirls,
While gulls dive-bombed like swirls.

When sandcastles start to twitch,
I swear they have a mind; what a hitch!
With a moat that looks so sly,
It gurgles like a sneaky pie.

As dusk settles and dreams arrive,
A fish tickles my toe to thrive.
With gentle laughs in warm refrain,
This island life is quite insane!

Unfurling Leaves in a Sea of Gold

Bright rays tickle my toes,
As laughter dances in rows.
Swaying palms in a silly breeze,
I forgot my flip-flops, oh please!

Sipping juice from a coconut,
Seagulls squawk, strut and strut.
A crab in glasses, what a sight!
Clapping claws in pure delight.

Sunhat flipped, a style faux pas,
I tripped and fell, oh ha ha ha!
Friends erupt in giggling glee,
Will I make it to the lea?

A skedaddle from pesky flies,
They're buzzing 'round with their own lies.
In golden light, we lose the hours,
Chasing ferns and sun-kissed flowers!

Dreams Adrift on Serene Waters

Waves are giggling, what a sound,
My boat's turned sideways, oh, I'll drown!
A dolphin jumps with playful flair,
I scream and splash without a care.

Floating dreams in a pineapple,
Sailors sing tunes like a chapel.
My oar is gone, it rolled away,
Time for a sun-soaked holiday!

Friends are trying to catch that fish,
But they mistake it for a dish.
It darts away with a cheer,
Laughing hard, oh dear, oh dear!

As time drips like melting ice,
We play in waters, oh so nice.
With every splash, another jest,
Who knew a boat ride could be blessed?

Palm-Flecked Memories of Pure Bliss

In golden halls of leafy shades,
Laughter hides in friendly glades.
A picnic spread, ants take a chance,
Stealing crumbs, they join the dance!

Tanned toes wiggling in the sand,
Caught a crab with a boogie band.
Sunglasses worn, but one's askew,
Hey, who put glue on my shoe?

Sunburned noses and silly hats,
Frolicking with friendly bats.
Each wave tells a joke, it seems,
We collect them like silly dreams.

With ice cream drips down my chin,
I smile wide, let the fun begin.
With palm trees swaying in the breeze,
Memories made are sure to tease!

Chiaroscuro of Daylight and Night

In bright beams I dance with glee,
While shadows hide and watch me flee.
A bird's shadow thinks it's sly,
But I catch it with a wink and a fly.

The moon takes a peek, says 'Hi there!'
While I sip coconut, not a care.
A sneak attack from a sneaky crow,
Crack me up, as the laughs overflow.

Sunset giggles, painting the sky,
Silly clouds float, I can't deny.
Laughter echoes, in colors so bright,
Making fun of the sleepy night.

With light as my partner, I tease and play,
In a world that shines, come whatever may.
Turns out the night can be quite a clown,
Whispering jokes as daylight goes down.

Dancing Shadows in the Ocean's Embrace

Waves are giggling, pulling my toes,
While shadows tango where no one goes.
I chase a crab, think I'm a pro,
But he laughs and scuttles, oh, what a show!

The breeze whispers secrets, tickles my nose,
A jellyfish floats, wears a hat of rose.
With every splash, the seagulls squawk,
Making me trip, oh dear, and walk!

Underwater twist, a fish sings a tune,
Telling tales of a clumsy raccoon.
A starfish claps, calls the audience near,
It's showtime, folks! Let's give them a cheer!

With shadows in dance and laughter in waves,
Every splash speaks of the fun it craves.
Even the sand loves to join in the spree,
As we spin and twirl, wild and carefree.

Treasure of Light Where Palm Trees Swirl

Pirate parrots squawk under leafy greens,
While palm trees sway, like they're in scenes.
A treasure map drawn in yellow sun,
Leads to a party — oh, what fun!

Coconuts roll, they're playing too,
With giggles and whispers, they're quite the crew.
Mangoes beam bright, yell "Come take a bite!"
And the limes just laugh at the fruit's delight.

Seashells gossip on the sandy floor,
While crabs crack jokes; who could ask for more?
A wave steals my hat, "Hey, that's not fair!"
But I just smile, with sun in my hair.

A treasure of laughter, where sunlight plays,
We dig in the sand on these funny days.
Every wrinkle and giggle tells tales of gold,
In a world where joy never grows old.

Speckled Rays on Sandy Shores

Sandy socks are the latest trend,
As footprints lead where giggles blend.
A sandcastle tower, with walls made of cheese,
And a moat of lemonade, if you please!

The rays come out, dance on my skin,
While seaweed sways like a goofy twin.
A beach ball pops, oh, what a sound!
And laughter erupts from all around.

With shells as microphones, we rock and roll,
As bubbles bounce, playing the soul.
The tide tosses jokes, waves roll with pride,
While I laugh and take my giggling stride.

By the evening's glow, flames tickle the night,
Yet still, we play till the stars shine bright.
With speckled rays and toes in the sand,
Life's just a joke, oh, isn't it grand?

Glimpse of Eden Beyond the Horizon

Golden spheres bounce in the blue,
Sipping drinks, we giggle true.
Turtles dance in dizzy spins,
While the coconut's shower begins.

Locals laugh at our failed tan,
As seagulls swoop down on our plan.
Crabs in tuxedos, what a sight,
Taking selfies, feeling light.

Waves with jokes, a playful tease,
We're like kids, just aim to please.
Sand castles with moats so grand,
Shattered by footfalls in the sand.

With each splash, the world seems bright,
As laughter echoes, pure delight.
Chasing shadows, having fun,
In this paradise, we have won.

Breath of the Tropics in Luminous Space

Fragrant breezes tickle the nose,
Bikinis, surfboards, and wild rose.
In fluffy clouds, we dream and sway,
Making up games we'll play all day.

Sipping drinks with tiny straws,
They slip and slide—oh, the flaws!
Fruit hats on heads add to our charm,
As we dance, we bring warm balm.

A pelican steals our lunch so sly,
We laugh and wave as he flies by.
Fishy jokes from ocean depths,
Even the starfish tell their quests.

We hop on waves, surfboards at hand,
Balancing dreams like grains of sand.
This silly world, with giggles neat,
A sunny life, nothing can beat.

Music of the Sunbeams and Tidal Rhythms

Laughter rolls like waves in tide,
As people dance, with pride they glide.
Bongo beats paint the air so sweet,
While laughing fish jump to the beat.

Hidden treasures, beachcombers grin,
Finding flip-flops, what a win!
Waves whisper secrets, tales untold,
As gulls perform, so daring and bold.

Little kids with wild red hats,
Trying to be friends with stray cats.
Each splash a note, a rhythmic cheer,
With every sunbeam, joy draws near.

In this wild world of drifts so bright,
Each moment glitters, pure delight.
A serenade of laughter rings,
As life, like ocean, always sings.

Azure Dreams Under Golden Canopies

Under blue skies, we flit and float,
Our picnic ended up as a joke.
Sandwiches seem to have vanished fast,
Blame the gulls, those sneaky pests!

Palm trees jiggle as breezes blow,
With funky dances, they steal the show.
Sunshine chuckles at our mess,
As we try hard to look our best.

Inflatable flamingos bob so high,
They watch us tumble, giggle, and sigh.
We race the waves, we backflip too,
In this realm, who needs a cue?

Every sip of juice a grand parade,
With silly hats, our escapade.
This vibrant world, our hearts embrace,
With joy stitched into every space.

Wings of Light in a Tropical Dream

Golden rays dance like bees,
They tease the waves with gentle ease.
A coconut falls, a funny thud,
Telling tales of the local bud.

Palm trees sway in playful glee,
Whispers of secrets from land to sea.
Laughter bubbles like fizzy drink,
As seagulls plot with a wink and blink.

Held by warmth, all fuss is lost,
Unruly hats, the ocean's cost.
Flip-flops scurry in sandy chase,
Each step a giggle, a grim disgrace.

Under a sky that's laughing loud,
We dance like kids, a joyful crowd.
With snacks that melt and drinks that spill,
Joyful chaos, we sip and thrill.

Elegance of the Shoreline's Glow

Dressed in colors, bright and wild,
The beach is ruled by every child.
With buckets tipping and laughter free,
Sandcastles rise as the tide goes flee.

A seagull steals a chip or two,
While old Uncle Fred gets caught in blue.
With sunburns patterned like a map,
He's more like art than a beachside chap.

Each wave a wink, each splash a joke,
They tickle toes and make us choke.
As fishing lines become tangled fate,
We laugh at the stories we narrate.

Even the crabs, they shimmy and sway,
Start a dance party at the end of the day.
Chasing the foam, we wave goodbye,
To the day's antics and a twinkling sky.

Imprints of Delight on Warm Sand

Footprints lead like a dotted line,
We follow them straight to a drink divine.
With straws like snakes, and ice that sings,
Tropical flavors and all the fun they bring.

Sandy toes and giggles abound,
As kids find treasures, the lost and found.
A beach ball bounces in a silly race,
While nearby, a dog plays its own base case.

Shells whisper secrets of the deep,
While sun hats start to tumble and leap.
The ocean's roar becomes a cheer,
In this wacky haven, joy is near.

As the day bows, the sky ignites,
With laughter echoing, oh what delights!
We dream in colors, bright and grand,
Leaving our marks on this warm land.

Enchanted Waters Beneath Flaming Skies

Twinkling hues in a glassy lake,
Frogs auditioning, make no mistake.
With a dive and splash, they steal the show,
And giggles rise with every throw.

Turtles bask like they own the place,
While a flip-flop wanders in a race.
Fish try to dance but slip and slide,
As laughter echoes across the tide.

Starlit signs and secret paths,
A crab in a tux with impressive spaths.
We cheer him on as he twirls about,
Our little legend, there's never a doubt.

As the canvas ignites with dusk's embrace,
We gather round, a joyful space.
With stories in waves and stars that twinkle,
We'll chant our dreams and laugh until we crinkle.

Azure Whispers of the Shore

Waves giggle as they dance away,
Tickling toes on a sunny day.
Seagulls squawk, making quite a fuss,
Stealing fries from a lunching bus.

Crabs in suits scuttle to and fro,
Waving their claws, putting on a show.
Beach balls bounce with a comical thud,
As kids squeal in the sandy mud.

Flip-flops flop, what a funny sound,
As laughter rings and joy's unbound.
A parrot sips from a coconut shell,
Cracking jokes that are hard to tell.

With sunburned noses and silly hats,
Everyone laughs at the playful spats.
As the tide rolls in, the fun won't cease,
Here's to the joy, may it never decrease!

Radiance Over Coral Reefs

Fish in bow ties swim with glee,
Waving their fins quite carelessly.
Stars under water, so oddly bright,
Bubble parties last all night.

A walrus sports a monocle grand,
Judging the dance moves of seaweed band.
Octopuses juggling shells with flair,
Making spectators laugh and stare.

Clams play cards with a sly old crab,
Betting on pearls with a bubbly blab.
Jellyfish glow, disco lights in the spray,
Making sure the strobe won't fade away.

Turtles in shades take a leisurely ride,
With laughter bubbles rising high and wide.
In this watery kingdom full of cheer,
The heartfelt smiles are all we need here.

Tropical Serenade at Dusk

Bananas swing on a breezy chair,
Mangoes gossip with a fruity flair.
The toucans croon their zany tune,
As nightfall slips in like a cheeky raccoon.

Fireflies twinkle in a comical race,
Buzzing about in a lightning embrace.
Pineapples giggle, hats on their heads,
While palm trees sway with dance steps in threads.

A party parrot paints the sky bright,
Wearing shades and wishing goodnight.
Coconuts chuckle at the moon's soft glow,
As everyone gathers for a silly show.

From dusk till dawn, laughter resounds,
With joy and fun, in these tropical bounds.
So bring out the drums, let's give a cheer,
For the night of delights drawing near.

Warmth Kisses the Ocean's Tongue

The waves play tag with the golden sand,
While flip-flops scatter across the strand.
A chubby seal performs a dive,
With antics that make the tourists jive.

Merriment blooms like flowers in spring,
As children laugh and the sea birds sing.
Drifting hammocks tied with goofy knots,
Swaying softly under rum drink spots.

Surfboards tumble, a comical sight,
As surfers shout, balancing just right.
An iguana basks, adjusting its shade,
Countless sunburns are soon to be made.

Giggling shells tell tales of the tide,
Of mishaps and giggles, never to hide.
So raise your glasses to the warm breeze,
And toast to the fun that puts hearts at ease!

www.ingramcontent.com/pod-product-compliance
Lightning Source LLC
Chambersburg PA
CBHW072130070526
44585CB00016B/1604